WHEN I SET THE SWEETGRASS DOWN

WILL FALK

WAYFARER BOOKS
BERKSHIRE MOUNTAINS, MASSACHUSETTS

WAYFARER BOOKS

WWW.WAYFARERBOOKS.ORG

All Rights Reserved
Published in 2023 by Wayfarer Books
Cover Design and Interior Design by Leslie M. Browning
TRADE PAPERBACK 978-1-956368-40-6

10 9 8 7 6 5 4 3 2 1

Look for our titles in paperback, ebook, and audiobook wherever books are sold. Wholesale offerings for retailers available through Ingram.

Wayfarer Books is committed to ecological stewardship. We greatly value the natural environment and invest in conservation. For each book purchased in our online store we plant one tree.

PO Box 1601, Northampton, MA 01061	
860.574.5847	info@homeboundpublications.com

HOMEBOUNDPUBLICATIONS.COM & WAYFARERBOOKS.ORG

"Creativity moves him from being a prophet crying in the wilderness into a poet-shepherd keeping watch over the vulnerable. Through these songs of praise, lament, supplication, and much more, Will shifts from his analytic mind into an analogic mindset, from factual to figurative language that moves truths into Truth. This Truth revealed through him, and thus to us, comes from Nature itself."

—GAIL COLLINS-RANADIVE, author of *Light Year: A Seasonal Guide for Eco-Spiritual Grounding*

"The keenly drawn observations Falk makes about the natural world are given muscularity by his ability to contend with the ecocide that threatens the webs of kin we have loved, turned into poetry, and yet repeatedly degraded and disrespected. Coyotes howl, deranged by terraformed landscapes. Bears pray. Light cuts and slices, refusing to repair what has not yet been mourned. And yet, Falk refuses to admit defeat, planting lyrical seeds in the cracks of heartbreak. These are poems like valleys. Wide enough to hold weather that exceeds our simplistic human moralities."

—SOPHIE STRAND, author of *The Flowering Wand* and T*he Madonna Secret*

"These poems are delicious and haunting. An erotic dance with nature that will lead you to love, grieve, and consummate your relationship with the earth. Falk's poetry tastes of moss, sand, stone, dew, and faith. This is wilderness poetry for the Anthropocene."

—MORGAN SJOGREN, author of *Path of Light: A Walk Through Colliding Legacies of Glen Canyon*

"These wise and heartbreaking poems often left me in tears for Falk is not just a keen observer of nature but a devoted lover of the more than human world. He demands we bear witness to the violations and sorrows inflicted on this earth--yet he also lyrically weaves us back into a renewed and intimate relationship with the wild ones, the rivers and the forests, and all that is. This is a beautiful and urgent book that I will return to each day for solace and guidance."

—PERDITA FINN, author of *Take Back the Magic* and co-author of *The Way of the Rose*

"When I Set the Sweetgrass Down" is unflinching in its honesty and eloquence. Will Falk is a poet passionately in love with the natural world and unwilling to look away when horrendous things are done to her. His courage and devotion breaks hardened hearts open into a deeper connection with this precious world, which is an essential remedy for these times."

—APRIL TIERNEY, author of *Memory Keeper*

ALSO BY THE AUTHOR

How Dams Fall

CONTENTS

PREFACE: FIRST, THERE'S THE WORLD

First, there's wind kissing your breast,
chills chapping your lips,
and frost on your sleeping bag before dawn.

First, there's salmon swimming upstream,
heron stalking blue-gill,
and grizzly bear brothers wrestling.

First, there's nimble,
clean water chasing over pebbles,
ice cracking in the warmth of Spring,
and sand dragging over desert floors.

First, there's the world.
Then, there's poetry.

For what is poetry
without the voice?
and what is the voice
if not for the world that makes the voice possible?

There is no poetry
without wind forming the breath,
without land to grow food forming the tongue,
and without water keeping the poet's mouth wet
when she speaks.

The natural world speaks the original languages in many voices.
Lyricism exists in November's first flakes finding still waters on a pond's face.
Ancient syllables are formed by old-growth forests
telling their stories in the passing of seasons.
The oceans' eternal rhythms are the music creating life.

Many of these voices are forgotten.
Some have fallen into the silent night of total extinction.
Some are drowned out by the screaming hallucinations we call "civilized life."

Others have their vocal cords
cut with chainsaws,
bruised by bulldozers,
and stopped with asphalt.

It is, after all, much easier to destroy those who cannot speak.

BECAUSE I'M IN LOVE

Summertime and I'm in love
with what's left of a forest.

She lures me from the hot sun
into the cool, delicious embrace
of her green and golden shade.

She sings more than a song.
With birds in her branches,
and the dancing of ten thousand leaves,
she composes a full siren's symphony
that carries with pollen and seeds
on a soft, smooth, gentle breeze.

She shares her traumas with me.
Echoes of engines, screaming saws,
and the unwanted advances
of axe-wielding deaf men.
A plague of ink disease
sweeping through chestnut elders,
leaving no one to care for
all the struggling saplings.

I learn she's lost so many loves.
Wolves and wood bison.
The humans who learned her language.
Ancient groves of old-growth giants.

Even as broken as her beauty is,
I tell her I'm inadequate, unworthy.

My tongue is not skilled enough
to kiss away her pain,
to lick the sweet xylem sap dripping
down the silver skin of red maples
and from her many wounds,
to speak the words necessary
to describe the pain hiding
behind the sugar in her syrup.

My fingers are not deft enough
to caress away the memories
of her many violations,

to draw her pleasure from the shadows
as often as she needs, as often as it takes,
to remember that there are still men
who want to learn to love,

to write verse powerful enough
to pierce the thickness
of her former torturers' indifference
so that they will never, ever do this again.

She responds with butterflies, bear cubs,
and the quivering legs of a speckled,
white-tailed fawn leaning on
her mother's strong flanks,
trying so hard to take her very first step.

And I know no matter how
inadequate or unworthy I think I am,
I will, I must try, too

because, of course, I'm in love.

AN OLD AUTHOR

Time is an old author.
She writes with wind, sunshine, snow.
She writes on ocean floors and stone.
She scribbles on my body,
rewrites my brain,
and tattoos poems—
smile line by smile line—
on my face.

Her words are not always beautiful,
rarely what I want to see.
Sometimes I try to argue with her,
tell her to shut up,
take her ink somewhere else.

But she's never wrong, never quits,
and simply does not care
about being correct.

Time,
I hope my weeping
and smiling always show—

like the best poetry,
like the growing lines on my face,
like the patterns cast
by sun, moon, and shadow—

only ever worries about being true.

WHEN I SET THE SWEETGRASS DOWN

Too often, these days,
I cannot make the sweetgrass meet the flame.

The fragrance is a borrowed prayer, anyway.

My ancestors fallen,
over a continent and an ocean away,
forgot how. Or, maybe
never knowing my great grandmothers,
I lost them, too.
And, neither Bridget, Christ, the Creator,
or even a common ghost ever answers.

Oh, yes, I constantly look to the heavens.
But, the moon is too far to hear.
The stars too beautiful to care.
And, the sun? Well, he's too busy
keeping everyone alive.

It's better to look to your friends.
So, I do and, on the other side of the glass,
a mother bear ignores the thorns
and shakes blackberries out for her cubs.

Her prayers are evident in the blackish blue stains
on her cubs' happy faces.

I didn't hear her say anything.
Just some blood in the fallen leaves
where the stickers got into her paws.

She looked at me for a moment
and nodded to a clearing in the bushes
where my granddaughter played with her cubs.

With no children, nor gods or goddesses of my own,
that little girl's hope haunted me.
I set the sweetgrass down
and turned back to my work.

Working, wading through my own thorns,
my sweat waters plants,
my blood feeds the soil,
the bile boiling in my stomach
is a language the land understands.

So, let my labor be my prayer
let my granddaughter see the scars
blackberry bushes ripped into my skin.
Let her taste those berries
and paint her skin blue with juice
instead of grief.

That's how the bears pray, anyway.

THIS AMERICAN SOLSTICE

Light, made stronger by the dark,
flows from the half moon,
and makes the long journey down
to dance with her bright kin, the flames
leaping from a thousand bonfires.

Druid whispers are almost audible
as they scatter from groves of ancient, murdered oak.
The whispers ride coffin ships and railroad cars
to diasporize across oceans and a continent
seeking the children of those
they once taught to understand.

Now, only the shadows comprehend.

And, where the shadows flicker,
stag heads shift into wolves
singing to the stars.
Stars gather into flapping eagle wings
descending into salmon tails
churning cold, emerald streams.
Streams swirl around strong trees
rooted in the land that creates all of this.

But, it's a different darkness, here,
on this American solstice.
The stories are difficult to recognize.
We are generations
and too many forgotten languages from home.

NEARLY-BLIND RUST BELT BLUES

No one warned me that the smokestacks,
skyscraper guts, and starless nights
could turn my gaze so steely.

Carp leapt from green water
to smack the flanks of coal barges
hauling the corpses of ancient ones
who never asked to be cremated.

The river carried iron and irony
to the gulf. Never before had water
been forced to participate so completely
in fueling an inferno.

It happened as slow as oxidation
until I was as rigid as a machine.
My vision frozen on things
no one was meant to see.

A great blue heron wrenched my gears.
With a flash of feathers,
she swung low,
dumped sugar into my gas tank,
and led me back to the river's
curls and curves.

I stood haunted by
all I now could see.
If it had lasted any longer
I might have had to wirebrush
the rust from my own eyes.

A DYING TRICKSTER'S LAST JOKE

A dying, mangy coyote ran along I-70
across the cold, Colorado prairie.

As fast as he was, he wasn't fast enough
to outrun the tiny mites stripping him naked
or to catch a little heat from each falling star.

When the stars burned out,
as he knew they always do,
he turned towards the highway
seeking the warm, diesel exhaust
the trucks leave in their wake.

He might have been looking for one last joke—
the kind he and his trickster kin have always played.

But, it must not have been funny enough
that an animal who had dodged
rifle-shots, semi-trucks, and cyanide
would finally die
because rodenticides meant for rats and mice
had so weakened his immune system
he could not fight off invisible mites.

At last, he got too close to the road.
A truck swerved. And, there was a crash.

That's where I saw this freezing coyote,
trembling and shivering, licking himself,
as he gathered his few remaining tufts of fur,
and wore them like a stained and shredded sweatshirt
he pulled off someone who did not survive the wreck.

WATER WARS

Dirty as they are, rivers back east,
are, at least, still full of water.

And, that's where I'd be heading
if I wasn't so thirsty.

Looking for springs,
all I find are dry dreams
stalking me across the desert.

In the mirage, I taste a scene,
as clean as iron in wine:
Somewhere in California,
a rusty, sunburnt sign
hangs over a vineyard and celebrates
a family insurance business's longevity.

The phrase, "through the Great Depression,
the Great Recession,
and seven wars"
is typed under the smiling faces
of long-dead men in uniform.

Maybe it's my own dehydration,
desiccating my peace of mind,
that makes me ponder my own longevity.
And, forces me to sweat
during these times of drought.

I don't know,
but the brown coats of sheep

are sprinkled like dust
on the tree-less voids
I heard someone call "hill-sides."

What once flowed through here
left cattle to settle like pebbles
in the washed-out roadbed.

The vultures are jonesin' winos
circling the vines.
By the time they get there
they'll only find raisins.

These water wars dry my vision,
leaving me to believe wet
is only an illusion.

That's not even blood
flecked on the feathers
of red-winged blackbirds
perched uneasily
on a barbed-wire fence.

WORMS SPEAK DURING WAR TIME

When they can afford to take time away from their busy lives
spent creating and recreating earth,
worms— wriggling through plastics,
carcinogens, and spilled, forgotten toxins,
with mouths full of crushed bones
and blood-soaked soil— say:
"If you want to hear the wars,
then you must let your ears shrink.

They must condense to the size of the guerillas,
all the little warriors fighting all the little wars
always and everywhere
in places invisible and in plain sight.

Only then will you hear the repeated assaults
rivers make on the pocked faces of aging dams,
the chemical drip-drops that sound like gunshots
during the invasions of the world's lakes,
or the tireless helicopter hum of bee's wings
hustling to help the flowers make love
and to supply rations of beauty for the war effort."

The worms should know, after all.

They've eaten the remains
of innumerable, unheard and unheeded wars.
They've shat what's left of a few battles won
and countless battles lost. They've brought
too many soldiers home to their mother.

If nothing else, when worms spit the dirt out,
the remind us: "If you're gonna win a war,
you must,
at least,
acknowledge that you're in one."

OUR RESIDENT SERIAL KILLER

There is a serial killer who lives in my town.
Every few days, my neighbors and I
pass the mangled bodies of his young victims
splayed on the side of the road
amongst the shredded tires, condom wrappers,
and malt liquor bottles filled with piss.

Sometimes he kidnaps a few people
and promises to share the results
of his experiments with the rest of us.
We got together and begged him
to cut his subjects' vocal cords first
so we didn't have to listen to their screams.
It was much easier to ignore our fear
when we didn't have to listen
to those who disappeared.

We stand in front of caskets
containing the victims he murdered
with the slow trickle of carcinogens.
We wonder when we'll be next.
We wonder how long it will be
until the embalmer will drain
the blood from our veins.

Meanwhile, the embalmer wonders if
our local murderer will poison her
with the same brand of formaldehyde
she has pumped into so many
of our deceased neighbors.

I'm scared and sad.

I rather like living in my town
despite the constant homicide.
People here are nice, very peaceful
and kind.

That doesn't seem to matter one bit.
That serial killer keeps killing my friends
and methodically murdering my family.
Sure, I have a few friends left, but
most I will never see ever again.

I decided yesterday that my neighbors and I
needed to stop our resident serial killer.
We had a meeting, politely shared our views,
and properly sought community-wide consensus.

"Every town has a murderer,"
some shrugged and said.
Others would definitely love to help
but they don't want to end up dead.

Most agreed that everything will be ok
because ours is a big enough town
that he can't possibly kill everyone.
And, at the end of the day,
some of us, at least, will undoubtedly survive.

After our meeting, the town serial killer
did his gruesome thing, again,
and I woke up this morning,
like every other morning while I've been alive
to learn more of my friends, my family,
and my favorite neighbors have died

FEAR OF FLYING

I can't remember whether
my flight left at 10:20
or when I gave up
on ever finding home.

Cruising at thirty-eight thousand feet
for four hours and six minutes
from Milwaukee to San Francisco
is the farthest I've been from the land.

Billowing white below me,
clouds gather with the warning
"whatever you do, don't look down."
And like the best prophets
they are burned away.

When the clouds clear,
I see the Earth is flayed.
She is bruised
and stitched with asphalt.
I see my lover in the hospital
after a terrible accident.
She is alive but deeply scarred.

Bumping over hills and valleys,
which are not hills and valleys
but what the pilot calls "turbulence,"
I tell myself it's only thin air.

I am dizzy and confused.
Another home vanishes

as Utah slides east beneath me.
It takes half an hour
to cross the entire state.
Half an hour,
where once I lingered
for eight years.

As the attendants prepare
the cabin for landing, my ears pop.
I fasten my seat belt
and try to return my heart
to an upright and locked position.

CAPTIVE LIGHT

Light does not lack
a capacity for violence.
Anyone who has walked through a city knows that.

The sun was never so intrusive—
even burning my ruddy skin.
Overindulgent, perhaps, but
the sun's touch is always intimate,
the sun always knows how to touch you
and some pain is worth being earned.

Anyone who's been on a good honeymoon knows that.

Those electric lights, though,
stalking darkness through the night,
strangling loose pupils to pop
with sudden explosions
of metallic, harsh whites.

Navigating bright traps, straining
to see the guidance provided by stars,
I forgive the lights.

It's the city that makes them so mad
and if not exactly mad,
maybe electric lights
are just like the rest of us in the city:
scrambling to get away.

MY PERSONAL GOLGOTHA:
A GOOD FRIDAY PRAYER

A late snow in early spring
and winter's resurrection
has driven me across
holy lands again.

Finding neither warmth
nor myself, I keep moving
and discover comfort in the friction
of my feet on the road.
The blisters have mercy
and drown out
the keening screams
of acid searing my gut.

Signs on the road
warn me to watch for falling rocks
and, watching for too long,
my eyelids are heavy
with more than sleeplessness.

The stones pile up.
Wakefulness is an avalanche
too heavy to bear.

The cramps in my back
express more than pain
at the hardnesses
of the beds I make.

The strain of this chosen yoke
of self-imposed exile
drags me over stones
producing tensions
in my specific forms of resistance.

My stench is not just
my distance from fresh water
but the stale sweat
produced in constant unsettlement.

The pilgrims I pass
tell me it's Good Friday.
That, at least, makes sense.

I wonder, if I just said the word,
made the tiniest motion
towards simple faith,

would I be saved?

The heavens remain silent.
Lions and lambs lie together
starving with confusion.

Empty gazes
pour from empty skulls
lining the lanes
of the paths I must take.

And climbing my personal Golgotha,
with no cross, no crowd,
no prayers of my own,
it's only the weight
of martyred forests
on my shoulders.

I hope the skulls,
the lions, the lambs,
all the lost forests,
and even the soldiers
hear me whisper:

Mother, forgive me,
for I know not what I do.

RIDING WEST WITH DOUBTING THOMAS

We are fingers in the wounds on the land
tracing interstates west, probing old scars,
and praying to the road ahead.

Many miles and several collisions ago,
we heard a soft sobbing on the breeze.
We pressed our ears to earth
and heard the soil moaning
with the soft groans of recent history.

Still, we doubted.

Now, the mountains send us visions
across bruised clouds in a freezing rain.
The wind blows flecks of blood on dark feathers
where red-winged blackbirds lament
from a naked branch in a roadside ditch.

We approach the Rockies,
propping up heavy skies
faithful as they have been forever.
They are the great spines of the Earth.

But, on the horizon,
the visions become broken backs,
railroad cuts and hot asphalt,
dynamite stacked as high as buffalo skulls,
and barrels of gunpowder
mixed with bone dust.

Riding west, when it all blew up,
we learned destiny
isn't something you manifest.
We pulled our fingers out.
They were muddy and red.

We doubted the land's pain, once,
but we do not doubt now.

FOUR BLACK BEARS

Four black bears form my heart and soul.
The Pennsylvania Department
of Conservation and Natural Resources
calls one a boar, one a sow, and two, cubs

because invasive Europeans
(I'm sorry, "Americans")
identify more with domesticated pigs,
with pork, (the other white meat)
than they do the bears
they killed, captured, and forced
to dance the slow waltz to local extinction
before cutting their own forests down
to build ships to sail here,
to misname this continent
after a lost Italian merchant.

One of the cubs
forming my heart and soul
died of starvation.

The other is diabetic,
living off of days-old pizza,
moldy donuts spilled from
small-town trash cans,
and plastic bags of Wonderbread
or whatever a local bear-lover
could afford to leave
in the woods behind his house.

Sometimes, when she is very lucky,
my soul's surviving cub's mother
finds a beehive, gives it to her daughter,
and I see the cub trying to spy
her dead sister in the sticky honey
she stretches like time and memories
between her paws.

But time and memories
do not work like that—
not for precious bear cubs,
and certainly not for me.

Time and memories
do not crystallize sweetly
for us to ponder slowly
or savor completely.

Time flows faster than rivers
devoid of salmon.
And, memories sour in
stagnant reservoirs
held back by concrete dams.

The mother bear and I are furious.
Not because food was so scarce
we tried to abort our young.
Bears, like most mammals,
like most humans who've ever lived,
of course, do this when food is scarce.

Not because we, ourselves,
are too malnourished to make any milk.
But because we know
sometimes never existing
is better than a life of constant suffering.

Mostly, though, I am a male bear,
a boar, a solitary creature,
a man wandering through dying woods—
desperately lonely, surly
and admittedly, self-consciously,
guiltily horny— wondering if ultimately

it would be better if it was too many people,
a mate, or a hunter who finally took me.

HIGHWAY OF TEARS

The moon won't rise on Highway 16 anymore.

The stars disappeared with her
when she hitchhiked the wet ditches
between home and being found.

Her bright smile could end the long twilight
of the lingering northern dusk.
Now, she only glistens in the shadows—
a glimpse of braided black hair,
girlish dimples in a backwards glance
before the poplar leaves try to hide her.

A few miles on,
a mother bear stalks the highway,
hoping for her favorite little pawprints,
or even just a tuft of her cub's black fur on a branch.

An approaching engine growls
and she scampers away
from the sour scent of predators
in their diesel trucks.

Not far away,
under a billboard shouting "MISSING!!"
we pass a broken young bear.
Her thick, brown shoulders
were scraped red and raw
to stain the asphalt with reminders.

The forests' weeping slows to sobbing,
a soft patter of rain on fallen leaves.
Warmth flees south
leaving tears to freeze to faces
that can only cry on billboards now.

"Christ, it's so cold"
are words the wind steals from my throat.
The prayers on my breath
turn from steam to smoke
and blow away to find the missing women.

They never return.

I am left to wonder: what world is this
where even prayers hardened by the chill
disappear?

SUBURBAN SABBATH

Sunday morning,
when the prayers began boiling in my belly,
I fled the ceilings and walls to find open sky.

But, the open sky was empty.

Either the eagles deserted us
or their perches, high in the pines,
were turned into hymnal pages
and replaced by crackling power lines.

The war hawks followed the eagles,
searching for lands where the fighting spirit
is more than just a ghost.

Mourning doves wept so hard for so long
that the high desert lacked the snowpack
to replenish their tears.

Only the magpies were left.
Those old street fighters and survivors.
Black and blue, bruised and bloody,

and beautiful.

My prayers spilled out, then,
to mingle with the magpies
picking through Saturday night's suburban kitsch,
the cracked plastic and broken bottles,
scraping the concrete and
scattering from toppled garbage cans.

An old magpie, with a chipped beak,
landed there in my prayers.
I held my breath, hoping she'd find a few worthy
to carry up to the Creator,
or at least to use in building her nest.

"Oh, I don't do that," she said.
"The Creator left with the eagles.
And, if not the eagles, the trees.
Twigs and sticks build better nests
than prayers, anyway."

SPRING SCENES

1. Moss

first steps in the forest
arriving from endless cities

boots beat on bulbous moss
garter snakes flee for the stones

it is not the
moss' hollowness
the snakes flee

it is my own

2. White Pine

pine needles on pine branches
wave in the wind
as hard to see as single hairs
on your girlish head

our vision blurs
with the difference
between you, me,
and the trees

3. *Identity*

we are not Christmas trees
we are balsam firs

Christ never came to these forests
but Christians did
they brought axes and saws

and paper

4. *Prayer of the Monarch*
Or "Will Dance for Food"

is it because our flight is so painfully
beautiful that you destroy
the flowers, the bushes and the blooms,
our food?

so we must fly farther?
so we must search and flutter
flutter and search
until color, herself,
falls with the dust
from our weary wings?

yes, we dance
but not for you
and definitely not
because there should be
dancing in the revolution

not like the bees, either
(they dance because
extinction is imminent)

no, we dance
because we're hungry
and we hope you'll notice

SPRING, NOW

The warmth was welcome before
it soured and began disturbing
Winter's rest.

Now, the world melts
and water that should still be ice
speaks the truth.

There is an insistence
in each drip and splashing drop
that mimics the slip and stuttering slap
of the wet and incessant,
bardic prophet's storytelling tongue.

When white snow browns
and purity muddies,
Spring rips the blanket
sheltering everything.

The land is revealed
wet, shivering, and naked.
Her sobs collect in puddles
and seasonal ponds.

Follow her into the sludge
and she'll show you
the bones in the slush.
Skeletons in Winter's closet.
You'll discover bodies burned,
sacrificial flesh boiled for oil,
a little more warmth,

and a few more hours of
lantern light
in the long, dark night.

The bones were ivory once,
when they were remembered.
Yellow now, and forgotten.

This is Spring, now.
She is an unwelcome, sloppy troubadour,
drunk on cheap wine because the water
is too dirty to drink and she knows
someone must keep singing.

GHOST MINNOWS

It was supposed to be spring.

But there were brittle whispers
through the scrub oak and sage.
Locust wings stirred, withered,
ticked, tock'd, and kept time
for an eternal drought.

A tang hung in the air.
Brown shadows shuffled on the ridgeline.
The forest knew there was fire
when the tallest trees tasted screams
— smoke on the wind— in their leaves.

Thirsty and alone as I was,
I didn't hear the crackling groans
above the hum of constant combustion.
I didn't smell what the trees tasted
until the sun burned the dirt,
scorched my face red, and said:

"the difference between dust and ash
is an undying flame."

I didn't know I was lost, either,
until ghost minnows in a dead creek
found me floating belly up,
in dust and ash, downstream.

I watched as their gills
fluttered with memories of rain,

and their silver fins flicked
only the rumors of snowmelt.

Those minnows saved me.
Then renewed their endless journeys
against empty currents.

It took me a long time,
watching the inferno's reflection
on a few scales of fish skin
to learn the minnows' lesson:

you're only dead if you forget.

SEARCHING FOR BRIGID

Imbolc.
Searching for Brigid, not in Ireland,
but in Nevada,
what the Paiutes call Nuwu land.

I almost saw her pale face
on the lingering morning moon.
There was a brogue, I could have sworn,
in the ravens' song
before they hushed at my approach.

I thought I heard Celtic spells
in the whispers the stars made
as they shimmered on the snow.

But, then I stumbled into a patch of splintered sage
where men had stretched a battleship chain
between two tractors and ripped up everything
the cattle wouldn't eat.

Rifle shots violated the peace
and shattered the silence
that moments before poured
from the canyon mouths.
Mars, god of war,
rose red as blood in the east
and threw his light like a spear
to pin me to the ground.

Paiute ghosts rose from the highway
that paved over their burial cairns.

They climbed over barbed wire fences
to demand which borders
my ancestors had crossed.

In a language I did and did not understand,
they reminded me that
this is not where my traditions were born.
And, if I found Brigid here,
I would never truly know.

Nevada is much too far
from my greatest grandmothers' Irish bones.

PRAYERS I SAY TO GAELIC GHOSTS

Mine is the voice of a man
who cannot speak,
speaking.

A dry throat that remains dry
even when watered
with too much whiskey.

My compulsion only stirs
the sounds of shadows sliding over gravel,
moonlight shuffling in the sand.

I seek to match snowspeak,
the lyricism in winter's first flakes
settling into still waters.

Hearing these ballads, sang before time,
I recognize, perhaps,
this is the only music possible.

WHALER BAY

There are no whalers in Whaler Bay anymore.

There are no whales, either.

The ancient verse sang by
the original poets of the deep
has ceased
drowned
under the hushing tune of harpoons.

Wading breast deep into the waves,
cold covers my heart
and the silence salts my wounds
far sharper than sea water ever could.

When the pain threatens to wash me ashore,
condemnation barks from selchidhs and seals,
invisible but not inaudible in a clinging mist.

Otters knock on wet, gray wood
picking through the thin, white bones
and sucking meat from broken shells.

The echoes fade and all is still
when a chilly anger borne by dark clouds
blows in hard from the past.

I am numb but still I shake
to the haunting sound
of wailing on the wind.

An ocean dying mourns her dead.

MACHINE BANSHEE

Two tom cats screech
through the window at my head.

Branches scratch with wooden fingers
at their own trunks in the wind.

The sky is falling hot
burned orange by city lights.

The wail of a distant train whistle
proves that even the cry of the banshee
is a machine now.

No sleep for me tonight.
I fold my bones up
under bed sheets.

The train whistles again
with the voices of ancestors.

Their bones are folded
in shallow graves
under transcontinental tracks.

No sleep for them either.

SEARCHING FOR TÍR NA NÓG

Green gives to gray
winter on the beach.

It is cold. Cold sprays,
cold fog, cold waves.

The bay is empty save for ghosts:
Kumeyaay shades, metal-headed wraiths,
and the reconstruction of a wooden
conquistador's ship.

Peering west from California's edge,
reflecting myself while the ocean
reflects Oisín,

I was pushed by a personal
gold rush, rumors of Tír na nÓg.

I was pushed by necessity, needing a place to go,
by ancient stories diasporizing me.

But, standing knee-deep
in water numbing my feet,
I can push no more.

DIGGING

Cold clay turns cold spades
digging on a cold Canadian day.

Rain falls from a stone-grey sky,
a moist ancient voice instilling
sweat with visions of history.

Reflections pool in the dirt
forming traditional hoops of water.

Lekwungen soil refuses to yield to a Celtic shovel
causing blisters in long-forgotten places.

Heaving muscles scream with memory
until the wooden shaft
scrapes the calluses off the past.

The pick-axe swings in the ancient arc overhead
through a heavy stench of dynamite and dust
in fallen mines and western railroad cuts
thudding into the earth
that stopped bullets in trenches
at Fredericks- or Gettysburg.

Trenches, then graves.
The dirt sifts to cover the freckled faces
of nameless paddy dead.

Metal scrapes rock, spade strikes boulder—
a pealing, mournful bell.

Unmoved for ten thousand years,
sinking into this ground forever,
the boulder knows everything

pulling on time, pulling on space,
pulling me into clay.

BELTANE PRAYER

It may be dangerous to beseech the sun
in times of drought.

It may be risky to seek his attention
when the holy wells have dried out
and people— who dragged fragments
of their Celtic fairy tales
across an ocean, over blood-soaked fields,
and into the desert— sparked a bonfire

and

burned the whole world down.

Still, Bridget or Patrick help me,
I trust to magic,
even misunderstood magic,
and ask for solar deliverance.

Sunshine,
igniting the horizon every morning
with harsh realities,
offers answers more dependable
than the old gods, or new, ever do.

In the afternoon,
at the height of his powers,
the sun hums over my skin
and burns my brown beard red.
Then, the difference between
simple sound and prayer disappears

on the speech of little lizard feet
skittering across the baked, fallen fronds
of a date palm tree.

It's just hard to hear
during this noisy Beltane week.'
Sunshine and little lizard feet
are not enough when I long
to soothe myself by imagining
any of us can remember any of our
starving ancestors' actual prayers.

The best I can do is weep
by a mine, a mission, and a massacre site
forgotten by the McSons and O'Daughters
of the immigrant diggers, builders, and killers.

Ghosts tell me that only amnesiacs
insist that traditions can be ripped
from the land who created them
and imported like whiskey
to drown the horror of the diaspora.

A different kind of banshee
clothed in coyote furs and eagle feathers
screeches that the Beltane weather
is not complicit in America's
gilded veneer.

Sometimes, though, when you're desperate
or drunk enough to forget,
it just seems that way.

THE ANACHRONISM HERE

Breaking trail for days uphill in slushy mud,
the mountain begins to whisper
Sisyphus.

The pregnant moose behind me reminds me
winter's only way is through.

When I finally make eye contact
with the boulder I must move,
I blink first.

His scars show
that he keeps time by erosion
and he's been here forever.

His moments are marked in snowstorms.
His clock ticks with the whole
lifespans of glaciers.

From all directions, his weight
pulls the world to him.
He is the sun whom aspen groves,
eagles, and swirling red maple leaves orbit.

Gravity grows heavier
as I approach him shoveling gravel
with a half-crack'd spade.

The shattered stones break his hard heart.
He feels the beige and brown,
gray-blue violence in the pebbles
I scatter around him.

After the drill strikes his face
and the sparks are killed in the rain,
I rake his remains over the trail
and wonder if I
am the anachronism here.

WITCH HUNTERS

Earth, mother of all gods and goddesses,
knows that, just because magic exists,
it does not mean magic is infinite,
omnipotent, or even independent
from the laws of physical existence.

She thought every one of her daughters
burning at the stake, shrieking for her help
proved this beyond the shadow of a hope
as a global inferno scorched those shadows away.

She thought the hurricanes she flung
at urban coastal cancers, the earthquakes she conjured
to shake her children awake, the squirrel
and shark saboteurs she recruited to wage war
on energy infrastructure were obvious indictments
of blind faith in the false idols encouraging us
to believe that even if we don't make it,

the Earth will.

Time and time again,
with each forest lost, each river damned,
each mountain toppled, she has been defeated
by the black sorcery of technologic necromancy.

Indeed, how could any animal—

whose lungs she never fails to fill
with the constancy of abundant oxygen,
whose heart beats in rhythm with her ballads,
whose tongue tastes the sweet waters
representing her 4 billion year devotion
to giving everyone life—

conclude anything other than that
she has always remained
completely faithful to her commitment?

No, the Earth, the original witch,
does not stand idly by while
whole species of her descendants
are cast into the abyss of oblivion.

She would save her daughters
if she wasn't already choking on the stench
of her own burning flesh, if her bloody wrists
weren't already shackled to a hacked-down tree
they had to murder to incinerate her.

She would if she could. And, she can,
if only we became brave enough
to stand up to the witch hunters.

AGAINST CREMATION

They cremated my grandmother,
placed her body in a propane-fueled furnace
and flash-baked her in a pan.
It was finished in a matter of seconds
and they swept her bone fragments and ash
into a clay urn.

The Catholic Church forbids the scattering
of ashes and requires
the incarceration of the faithfully incinerated
in cemeteries.

My grandmother's mausoleum
was built from blocks of limestone,
the bodies of old boulders.
Limestone was built from the skeletal remains
of marine organisms,
the bodies of old oysters.

Block on block, body on body,
the stacked corpses of stone
surround my grandmother's ashes.
Little air, and less sunlight, gets in.
The dead house the dead.

The stone-cutters and mausoleum builders
cremate the grandest mother, Earth, too.
Millennia are geologic seconds,

and in a matter of decades,
with the flip of a propane-fueled switch,
Earth, my grandmother,
is flash-baked in a pan.

In these times of burning,
I beg the undertakers:
Please don't incinerate me.
Don't bury me in a casket,
and don't, whatever you do, embalm me.

Place me on the soft moss of a living forest
where rain and starlight will fall on me.
Let the wind scatter me,
decayed cell by decayed cell.
Let tree roots soak in my blood,
wrap me up and crack my bones.
And, if I am to burn at last,
let it be by the sun,
so that I may turn
not to ash, but to soil.

AMERICAN DREAMS

With American roads my only home,
I often make my bed on floors
and different floors give different dreams.

Despite the revolutions, many floors
are still made with deforested pine boards.
It's hard to sleep on chopped limbs and piled bones,
the broken bodies of dethroned wooden kings
and never again evergreen queens.

I long for silence or even just
a few moments' dreamless rest.
But these floors stacked on the stolen labor
of those bent by their right to work
have so much to say.

With no pillow to soften the nightmares,
my ear is not to the ground;
it is on the planks where saws feed
and beyond the wailing are screams
far sharper than steel.

The spray of orange sawdust
paints over the emerging greens of baby trees.
Fresh blood spills into previously pure snow.
Crimson seeps with shock into cream.

And, seeking too long for peace
in the uneasy sleep of this American dream,
I finally rise and flee for night.

Stepping into shadow beneath Colorado hills,
I know I am a stranger out here.
I have lived too long under
the violence of electric lights
and the hollow oppression
found in vacant rooms.

Then welcome fills the darkness—
the sudden lift of black wings
as a turkey leaps from the forest floor
and lights upon a branch
in the full glow offered by a full moon.

her laugh is liberty's lullaby.

She sings that my bed
can be a floor of living soil.
A warm breeze might drape
starlight's silver blanket over me.

And, if I trust the turkeys enough
to attempt sleep again, I will learn that
no matter what the dead men said:
all dreams are not created equal.

SKELETONS IN THE WATER CLOSET

We always thought America
held his liquor well.
He concealed his secret
genocides-and-tonics,
war old-fashioneds, and
dry massacre martinis so well.

But, this year, it's been bad.
You can find him
wandering around the West
tipping up bottled rivers
and licking the reservoirs dry.

There were rumors, even,
that someone saw him trying
to ferment a mine's tailing pond.

What we know for sure, however,
is that we're finding skeletons
in those water closets,
at the bottoms of those artificial lakes.

After filling them with toxic shit for years,
America was surprised to learn that
reservoirs don't flush.

He thought no one would ever find
the bones of trafficked children,
the dried-up murdered streams,
the remaining teeth of
the junkie vet who killed for pay,

was killed for pay,
and then dumped by a country
who thought he'd never be missed.

We tried to get him to listen,
to maybe just accept
that he really does have a problem.

But, as we watched water levels
hit rock bottom and saw
the Ghosts of Generations
Yet to Come rise from
the skeletons in America's closets,
we knew America would never quit

unless someone forced him to.

THE PORNOGRAPHY OF DESPAIR

Chained by the convenience of our learned helplessness
and convinced of our inalienable right to pleasure,
men shrivel and shrink in the frigid comfort
of air-conditioned rooms.

The dysfunction is cowardice. We sit idly by watching
while chlorofluorocarbons and other chemical penetrations
tear holes in the ozone membranes
protecting the fruitful intercourse of the earth and sun.

Oh yes, we always seem to see breasts.

But these breasts injected with silicone,
dioxin, and other carcinogens,

these loveless performers kept hard
by the desperation of women,

these plastic infections of orgasms
fabricated by phone and computer screens,

create the pornography of despair.

We know that it's much easier to get off
on the manufactured fantasies of our own powerlessness, now.

Fantasies never have been, never will be, enough.
Sooner or later the Freon of indifference
keeping closed hearts cool and sheltered from the sun,
will be prohibited by scarcity and the courts of natural law.

Please, my brothers,
pull your desire from that electric outlet in the wall.
Flush that Freon from your veins.
Step into the unmediated heat of summer sunshine
and let her searing wisdom remind you
what your manhood is truly for

SUICIDE AND OTHER EXTINCTIONS: A TRIPTYCH

Part I. Chorus Frogs

Though chorus frogs are gorgeous singers,
I hear they are going extinct in the Sierras.

I can believe it, but I don't.

They are not going extinct.
They are leaving, like you would
if you were a gorgeous singer
and no one was listening.

Part II. Star Fish

Whispers collect and recollect
in Pacific tidal pools where I wander
the cold beaches on the edge
of my own extinction.

The sea bends to wash the wounds on my feet.
The salt stings somewhere deep,
deeper than simple cuts and blisters.

I cock my head with the gulls
and listen to the details:
waves dragging driftwood,
crabs treading water,
terns skimming damp sand,
and then the gentle fragmentation of starfish
pulling apart, slipping away,
an entire species dying

one
limb
at a time.

I followed the scientists' whispers here,
goaded by rumors of what they call
"sea star wasting syndrome."

The scientists don't know why this happens.
But, I do.
There are too many devils in these details.
They speak so softly it's hard to understand.

The starfish aren't wasting; they're going away.

Part III. Me

Late one winter night, a dead chorus frog,
a sea star ghost, and I stayed up talking.

They told me you can find heaven
even in a pile of frozen dead bodies
with big shit-eating grins.

Death is a tundra wolf pack
watching a sick moose, they said.
Whether or not they catch you,
or find you collapsed on the ice,
they ask the same question of everyone:
 "Are you ready?" and then they watch
as your answer freezes to your face.

I did not understand until
the dead chorus frog sang:
"Hell is a pile of frozen dead bodies

frowning."

ANTHROPOCENE WRITER'S BLOCK

Sometimes when I sit down to write,
visions rise from the paper.

Desperate men come for me.
Sometimes, they crack my head open
to see what's inside.
Other times, it's a slow parts-per-million poison,
that they're sorry,
but, let me assure you,
they never knew was harmful.
The best times are the quick, painless injections
that leave no mark
and don't affect my market value.

They turn my skin into leather,
and design exotic shoes for expensive parties.
They stretch me across cushions,
take afternoon naps, and always ignore their dreams.

They line their jacket hoods with my hair,
which keeps wind from whispering in their ear,
keeps winter from touching
cozy hearts in sheltered chests.

One of them, especially creative,
builds a xylophone with my bones
and plays the dirtiest,
the funkiest,
the sickest beats, ever
for the ones tapping their toes
in my skin shoes.

It's hard to blame them.
They're just creating beauty, after all,
And, if not beauty,
they're just doing their jobs.
There's rent, other bills,
food on the table,
and we all gotta eat,

don't we?

When the xylophone fades away,
and the couch is finally refurbished,
I see the murdered tree
in the paper in front of me.
My burning skin and sore bones
wonder what chemical scribbles
I can tattoo on this tree's flesh
that would bring the tree
back to life,
so she could forgive me.

SUR-REALITY

Surrealism turned into surreality
as the biosphere was microwaved
like left-over soup.

The machine hummed, the timer counted down,
and while I studied my plastic reflection
in the microwave door,
I wondered if my mushy mind
was the product of a brain tumor
grown by the radiation I ignored
or was manufactured by my fear
of the machine's final, inevitable beeps.

My mirror image could not discern
the despair there in my softened mind,
could not judge my soul for reaching
for long dead deities.

No, not Christ.
I've re-heated too many dishes
that I swore the night before were heavenly
only to find the divine
does not survive even a brief nuking.

Food is life
and stale food always reminds me
that I have no desire for eternity.

Maybe the Buddha.
Though I think he was a lot like me.
Just constantly lost.

His soul was supposed to be
reincarnated in the age of Google Maps.

He wasn't. So, he leaned into it,
and said fuck it, might as well
make a world religion out of it.

Reality, hit me then. Not the flirtatious love-tap
of a kid on the playground. No,
she smacked me with that
spring-loaded microwave door,
probably where that tumor was growing.

With a lumpy head and overheated cheese
the consistency of concrete,
Reality, that beautiful daughter of Earth,
as strong and cold as arctic ice floes
ditched her sur-, opting for the single life,
to shatter the fantasies of men.

I think I'll worship her.

MALADAPTIVE BEHAVIOR

When I feel crazy or run out of things to say
(as if there really is a difference),
I wonder why I even bother
to write all of this down.

When I feel crazy or run out of things to say,
I go to Thacker Pass.
I like to find a warm, flat stone
to sit on and read and think.

One time, I took the psychologists' bible,
the Diagnostic and Statistical Manual, fifth edition,
with me.

In the DSM V, I read that talking
to a rock is atypical, not necessarily pathological.
When a patient believes the rock is talking back, however,
that is maladaptive behavior.

I set the book down and remembered a time
spent in the mental hospital when
my doctor summed it up like this:
"It's ok to speak to stones.
It's when they speak back
that you should be worried."

But there are no doctors in Thacker Pass.
There are no patients, either.
There are, nevertheless, countless chatty stones.
And, they told me to write all of this down.

SOMEONE ELSE'S MAP

in the havenwoods, a different gossip
is discernible from bird-talk
it comes from the paisa, the fairies of the forest

the paisa speak of a young Meskwaki woman
who felt her way through the trees
chased by cartographers
wielding the sharp points of compasses

exhausted and lost, stuck and desperate
she lay down on the bluff
overlooking the beyond

ripped naked on a red granite ledge
under a full wolf moon
exposing ink lines of latitude
and longitude tattooed on her bare flesh

with contour lines crowding her nipples
and place names stitched
on her valleys and curves
in invasive English
this young Meskwaki woman was
someone else's map
someone else's breasts
someone else's sex

the paisa think the course was predestined
when located by her navigators

she leapt
from the bluff
flapping and tattering
no longer to be read

MEN ON A STRAWBERRY MOON

When I could no longer ignore her,
I met the June moon's gaze.
Pink, full, glowing
with the lush sweetness
of freshly picked strawberries.
She transfixed me
with silver stakes of truth
to the face of a rolling planet
frantically trying to turn away.

The astronauts blamed her
as they always seem to do.
"She was asking for it,"
they shrug and say.
"If she didn't want us
to stick a limp flag in her,
she wouldn't have looked
so damn good."

Earth tried but I could not—
would not— look away.

The moon responded to my refusal
and poured searing enlightenment
into my sore mind.

It had nothing to do with strawberries,
how she shined, or whatever light
she chose, that night, to wear.

No, her feminine power
had simply existed
for too blessedly long
beyond the grasp of men.

And they never can tolerate that.

When she finished pulling tides
of tears down my face,
she reminded me that power derived
from trying to keep a woman
or a planet in her place
may seem for a while to wax
but always, always wanes.

ABORTING TRUTHS

With so many stillborn,
I have to wonder:

How many truths are aborted?
Before we get it just right.
Before one arrives writhing
and wringing wet,
kicking and screaming,
promising to destroy the world
of fantasy everyone forsook
reality for.

Should we practice safe speech?
Rubber our mouths?
Suck down pills to shed veracity,
bleed away honesty,
when we feel it kicking
in what we thought was
the barren womb of our soul?

Is life today so good that
we are afraid of curse words—
curse words like
"choice"?

Or, do we forget that
you and I were never asked
if we wanted to be here?

When, most of the time,
we don't.

WINTER WIND

No one to kiss tonight but the winter wind.

A demanding lover -
cold and jealous, bright and beautiful -
she pulls me from my blankets
into the sky.

When, at last,
my lips are chapped and cracked,
she rewards my fidelity
by blowing shooting stars west
after the sun, who, long ago,
vanished. Then, she leaves.

And, I am left to ponder whether
the stars I wish upon
do, in turn, wish upon me.

LOOKING FOR A GOD?

Looking for a god?
the stars ask
why not us?

We're always there
whether you see us or not.

We're infinite
the sleepless can tell you.

We do not rule by force
but through the charisma
in freely offered splendor.

Instead of ten,
we have one simple commandment:
don't drown us out
with smog and smoke
with false gods and pretenders
with city lights and ceilings.

Keep the earth and sky clean,
and the darker things get,
the worse things are,
the harder we will try
to tip your face
gently to the sky
and shower you softly
with shimmering kisses
and silver blessings
no matter your supposed sins.

SHARING THE MOON'S GAZE

Half a moon
looked at all of me
even though she was
surrounded by stars.

I was too coy
so a jet plane
dragged a curtain of clouds
across her face
while she checked me out.

I knew she was into me
as the strength of her warm light
painted a rainbow across
the cloud curtain's tail.

Showered in her golden attention,
a sigh of the simplest pleasure
left my lips
just as an owl hooted
his version of an avian moan.

I made eye contact with that owl
and he was as surprised to see me
as I was him.

He quickly, properly
straightened and smoothed his feathers,
swung his head away and leapt
to let the wind
wash the longing from his wings.

And I learned she looks at all of us
like that.

MERCURY IN RETROGRADE

Astronomers tell astrologists
that retrograde is an optical illusion.
Planets do not move backwards.

But it is easy to be fooled
when it is easier to accuse
celestial bodies than those
who break, beat, and bash
Earth's body in front of our
starry eyes.

It's not that the sun,
the moon, and the stars disagree
that they exert an influence
on your life.

Sunburnt skin,
pale, pasty, bloated bodies
drowned in rising tides,
staring blankly at the moon,
and anyone who has tried
to find the stars despite city lights
can tell you that.

The planets will tell you, however,
that the sun burns hotter
because a hole has been ripped
in Earth's atmosphere.

The oceans swell
with the sweat of a feverish world
long-infected with spiritual viruses,
delusional hope, and
the rejection of plain reality.

Mercury, so often blamed,
is busy being the messenger of the gods,
and simply does not have time
to turn back, to switch his spin,
to truly be in retrograde.

He may pause, though,
for just a moment, to remind us
who it was that built those city lights
that stifled the stars, in the first place.

So the sun, moon, and stars
watch the murder of their sister,
Earth, and gently suggest:

It might not be optical illusions
causing your grief, exhaustion,
and stress.

WHEN WHALES SAVED MY LIFE

Reaching for relief from pain, insomnia,
or everything that's happening,
sometimes more than the recommended dosage
of little blue pills spills out onto my palm.

There they sit.
                        Monolithic.
Heavy with ancient temptations.
Cairns on the trails
running across my hands.

They point to a different way—
a way out, perhaps,
or just a way through.
The straightest path to somewhere,
anywhere else.

My hand trembles like it's been stung,
but I will not drop them.

I watch the pills, fascinated.
Small promises, little whispers,
tiny, tiny offers
          of peace
                        at last.

I have been here before and
I know where that cairn'd path leads;
the cold beds where these little blue
albatrosses settle.

The first steps can arrive
so light, so easy.

And then,
                         your words drop through.
Sunlight piercing cold depths.
Echoes over the long distance
between warmer times.

Whales,
you said in your singer's voice,
make the oceans healthier
just by being whales.

They swim strongly, freely
from the cold below
to the surface to breathe.
Being whales, like this,
they mix the waters up
and deliver the ocean's vitamins.

All the way down here,
where the cold water numbs,
and sound threatens to drown,
I hear your song, like a whale's,
and I put all the pills away.

All the pills—save one—
the most important pill of all:

my medicine for cowardice.

THEY CANNOT SWIM IN YOUR TEARS

There are ten vaquita porpoises left on Earth.

Though the nets of extinction grow ever tighter
around the world's tiniest marine mammals,
their bright eyes still twinkle
where sunshine reaches through the waves.

Despite the roar of boat motors
on the wind and under water, they still smile
as the taste of oxygen is made ever sweeter
by the knowledge those boats drag in their wake—
the knowledge that each gulp of air
might be each porpoise's last breath.

Fishermen curse as they pull in their nets.
They gingerly lift the rough twine
biting into bloody vaquita flesh.
The lacerations cut deeper and deeper
as the vaquita thrashes in desperation for release.

These fishermen are familiar with suffering.
Fish are harder to find.
Wider nets must be cast.
More boats crowd the delta than ever before.
And, their children still can't feed themselves.

So, they know what to do
when they witness a vaquita's eye
rolling frantically in pain,
when there's little blood left
to spill across the boat's deck.

One takes the porpoise just above her tail fin
and whips her through the air she was enjoying
before the motors arrived.

High overhead, first, and then violently down
to mercifully smash her skull
against the boat's metal siding.

It's not unlike the way soldiers,
after grunting that nits make lice
or muttering something about following orders,
take shrieking toddlers by their ankles
and permanently silence them
against a stone, tree, or unfeeling concrete.

It's easy to believe, when your heart
breaks like a stoved-in skull,
that the nets of grief will drag you down
to drown in depths of darkness
next to a broken porpoise carcass.

This belief is bolstered by the fact
that your tears taste like the ocean's.

But, the porpoises promise,

if we do not stop the next hand
reaching for tail fins or another shrieking toddler,
then your grief, their grief, our grief
will only get worse.

There are still nine vaquita porpoises left on Earth.
And, tiny as they are,
they cannot swim in your tears.

DREAMING GOD

I lost myself somewhere
between here and home.

With no one to listen,
I ask God for guidance,
and only the local poets answer.

Instead of direction,
they point long forefingers
at the skinny hints given
by a freshly broken branch.

They whisper ashes in the wind
and reveal the vanishing meaning
in the disappearance of an owl's tail
towards darkness.

When the poets go dry with silence,
stirrings in the waterless dirt
chastise me for my lack
of healthy disbelief.

God was only a poem, after all
dreamt up long ago
by a lost and lonely shepherd
struggling to cope with a cold Hebrew night.

That shepherd materializes
in the smoke of my prayers.

He clutches to his rough-hewn staff
bearing it like a cross
because prophets in poets' clothing
took the last of his flock.

While we smile weakly
across the millennia at each other,
it helps to think we're not too different
that ancient shepherd and me.

The stones are a hard but familiar bed.
The stars are still too numerous to count.
And the night is always long.

Shivering like this, we dream God,
talk to ourselves, and try to keep warm.

DESERT PROGNOSIS

Wrapped in the dark blanket of night,
huddled and feverish with cosmic infections,
either I'm shaking or the sky is.

I look to the heavens with so many wishes.
But, there are only so many shooting stars.

The last star is erratic, bouncing off her sisters
before she tails away and burns out.

Witnessing this, I find it easy to confuse
planes with proper prayers
and machines with meaningful magic.

When the smoke runs out,
and I have nowhere left to go,
I retreat into sleep,
the cheapest anesthetic available to me.

The moon rises but she is too bright for sleep.
Finding me awake, she attempts to explain it all to me.

The fullness of her pale light
cannot pierce the dense ignorance of my darkness,
so she sighs, and pulls the clouds across her face.

Then the coyotes begin.
One sings, one whines, one laughs and one
is on the scent of the way on.

I hear but I can't remember how to listen.
It's not the cold, but my own deafness
that causes me to shiver.

Just when I'm about to add
the loss of language to the list of my afflictions,
a nighthawk's wing brushes the tears from my cheeks,
and I know the birds, at least, will cry with me.

LOST SLEEP

Bears go to bed when the land does.

The land collects frost to knit into blankets of snow,
and somehow the bears know
to slow down and find their dens.

Each year, the frosts arrive later.
Winter's quilt, heaped in tattered piles
and stretched too thin across the land,
threatens to vanish.

This year, the frosts never come.
There's not enough fabric
for the land to weave her bedspread.

On a warm January day,
not a crow, but the shadow of a crow
passing over old snow,
black with dirt and mud,
muttered that he can lead me back to the cold.

I followed that crow to an evergreen grove
where the wind twitched with whispers
of the violence of a Spring
angry for being disturbed so soon.

The crow landed in a hillside pine
and sang a dirge for the distended belly
on the corpse of a soon-to-be mother bear.

I don't think it was the tears in my eyes
that convinced me the trees huddled
around the bear and her unborn cubs.

With no sheets of snow,
or even sleet to work with,
the land begged help from the trees.
Together, they gathered shadows
to wrap the dead bear in
and freezing forever like this
she caught up on seasons of lost sleep.

THE MORNING AFTER

(Or, that time white archaeologists
realized people have been in America forever)

The morning after
Halloween
when the sugar subsides
and the paint no longer
hides us from ourselves
the ancestors still whisper

some moan, some scream
and some keep trying to treat
with these generations
that fell for the trick
that ghosts are supernatural,
that spilled blood seeping into mud
isn't powerful enough to preserve
the reality of their suffering
forever

the ancestors still whisper
whether we hear them or not
when the veil is thick
or the veil is thin,
the massacred and murdered resist
that artificial saccharine buzz
drowning everything out

THE GUN THAT WON THE WEST

The same day the Marlboro Man died,
a 132-year-old, 1873 Winchester repeating rifle
was found leaning against a gnarly old juniper tree
in Great Basin National Park.

The news proved that some ghosts refuse to die.

No one knew who left the gun there.
But, then again, no one asked the juniper
who would tell you of a veteran of the Snake Wars
who got sick of shooting at snakes
when Paiutes were all he would kill.

In a gun magazine, a man celebrated the discovery.
He was excited because this rifle
is the firearm that earned the name
"the gun that won the west."

Apparently, the Winchester repeating rifle
"probably killed more deer, more buffalo,
and more Indians"
than any other weapon in America.

I don't smoke but suddenly I craved a cigarette.

In my craving, I saw the holiness
in the way wildfire smoke curls around the earth,
wreathing us all in the prayers
of a planet that simply wants to stop burning.

There are nights, on the eve of war,
when I wonder if cigarettes save lives,
if the Marlboro man was simply misunderstood.

In a suicidal and cowardly culture,
despair makes it difficult to act.
Pulling the trigger is too dramatic.
Or, hands shaking with fear,
we shoot at ourselves and miss.

Cigarettes, the Marlboro Man tells us,
let us kill ourselves one drag at a time.

THE VIEW FROM SENTINEL ROCK

Winter is late again after another long summer.

The drought blows through and January mocks us.
The sky is dry, filled with cottonwood pollen
cruelly mimicking snow.

Below Sentinel Rock,
where "nits make lice" the soldiers said
and newspapers reported
the now "permanently friendly Indians"
took an "astonishing amount of lead,"

I cannot look the Rock in the eye.
She's seen too much.

The mercury mine has long since bled out
and the only evidence of violence
is a mining corporation's weather station.
The planet's thermometer threatens to shatter
while the station's anemometer spins faster.

Sage brush holds each other up
huddling together in the wind.
Pinyon pines have long since succumbed,
but a juniper clings forlornly on.

Naked aspen tremble in the cold
and reach their bare limbs
towards blankets of snow
that were infected long ago.

The shades of miners linger
whispering in the dust dragged over hot gravel
in the parched bed of the unquenched Quinn River.

They water their horses
in the murk of a tailings pond.
The horses are blind from the black.
They were worked too hard underground
and now their milky eyes are wrapped in gauze.

With no gauze or other blinders of my own,
I turn away seeking a better vision.
Instead of answers, I find a dead deer
collapsed across the trail.

No bullet holes, no blood, not even a fly.
Only blank, pewter eyes
fixed on Sentinel Rock offering honest reflections,
refusing, even in death, to look away.

WARS MIGHT BE DIFFERENT NOW

Shadows surrender to the east,
withdrawing from Mauna Kea
back to the sun's warmth this morning.

The waning moon, above the garrison,
at the US Army's Pōhakuloa Training Area,
offers no heat, just something to watch.
Her comrades, the stars,
send what light they can.

The sun begins to rise
and I huddle under a thin blanket
praying that a few strong stars
will hold on.

From the west, stillness is interrupted
by rifle fire in the valley below.
The breeze wakes with the dawn drills
and stirs the Hawaiian flag
hung upside down.

The pops and rattles grow stronger
mixing with the flag's snaps and furls.
The soldiers gain ground. Then,
the rumble of mortar rounds.

"Howitzers," the uncles say,
wincing through the blue smoke
their cigarettes make.

Mamane trees tremble
and a gold flower shakes loose
falling into boot-tramped mud.
'Ahinahina try to bloom.
But they learn it's been a long time
since flowers stopped a war.
And, they draw their silverswords.

With our trenches dug,
and little left to do, we wait
and hope the mountain's slope
slows the vanguard's pace.

The slowness of the clouds
under the sky's pacifying blue
tempts me into thinking
wars might be different now.

The last twinkle in the sky
suggests it's not my blanket,
it's my courage that's worn too thin.
I cling to that flash of silver in the gray.
It says this occupation will never quit.

But neither will the stars,
no matter how dark it gets.

AS TRADITION GOES UP IN SMOKE

When the frost of ancestral protection
vanishes with rising temperatures
and minds grow soft with amnesia,
they come in heavy trucks
to mine memories and steal stories.

Glaciers remain, for now,
wavering, with teardrops melting from their faces,
as tradition goes up in smoke.

Tall pines huddle together to share their secrets
before the tornadoes strike.
Eagles, crowned gold or white, float on the future,
interceding with the Creator,
begging blessings for us from on high.

The air is full of a winter's anger.
North winds blow resolve.
Clouds try to freeze themselves,
fall to Earth, and pack themselves as snow.

It's not until we face the trucks
that the Creator notices the eagles,
and She rises from the union
of icy rain on sage.

With drum in hand and magic in her throat,
She is silhouetted, before dawn,
against a red warning sky.

Strong, dark, and tall
her raven hair flutters with whispers
and the ecstasy of southbound geese in flight.
She is a shining morning star
guarding the wonders of night
from the conquering electric lights.

Her song freezes our muddy memories.
The glaciers smile. The eagles rest. The trees relax.

And, the miners' shovels snap and crack.

GREAT BASIN DAZE

The clear days are the worst
and, here, every day is clear.

Skies, blue with utter boredom,
let the sun pour down at cask strength
and the hours move so slowly
they must be drunk.

The wind finally stumbles in
followed by the first flicker
of wildfire sparks scorching senses of smell.

A pinyon jay sneezes
where she huddles in the half-shade
dried-up sage struggles to maintain.

The scent reminds her of the days
when rabbit brush bursts into flames
signaling the ripeness of pine nuts.

A Chilean shepherd leans
against a camper trailer,
spooning something syrupy
from an aluminum can,
while pondering a reflection
of the Andes
in Nevada's Snake Range.

No one but a pronghorn,
haunted by ancestral memories
of rifle cracks and echoing bullets,
notices the pioneer ghosts
who pick through cattle bones
for beef that rotted decades ago.

GREAT BASIN WAYS

The Great Basin has her ways
of ripping the tissue off scars
that hem you in like barbed wire
cattle fences on public land.

She reaches from the sky
with fists formed of snow and ice.
She scrubs you raw
against ranges of exfoliating sage
and leaves you naked on mountain tops
to be purified by the night.

Then, she cuts you open
with sharp winds, a sickle moon,
and stars stabbing down,
to let your infections drain with the dust
through rabbit brush, rat caches,
and down a mouse hole.

She calls her coyote children
to catch your scent.
They yip and yap
and cackle with glee at the witchcraft
she works in your transformation.

Their paws dig you up,
their teeth pull you out,
and their rough red tongues

lick you clean
until you fall, face first,
covered in canid spit
into the frost and cow shit
fully yourself again.

WHERE TO GO

In the canyon, where I wander,
I wonder at the emptiness of it all
and forget where to go.

Burnt orange reaches to blue
where the stones hold the sky.
The strong hands of stones
are the only hands sure enough
to carry the sky.

Then, the wind blows and the stones sing.
The melody plays on orange rock formations.
The stones' thick, tall fingers
crack in time, snap with a rhythm
that knocks me flat on my back.

These stone hands stack
the rock of my skull
on the rock of the canyon floor.
The bones of the desert
crisscross with the bones of me.

Bone on stone, stone on bone,
we are made into a cairn.

And, in the stacking, I am cracked open,
and poured out, pooling with the shade
against canyon walls.

And, in the cracking, the canyon
is no longer empty. It is filled with me.

As the sun sets, and the sky
turns a heavier black, the stones give me back
to myself. I stand up and look around.

The canyon shows me
the remainders of a cairn
and I remember: that's where to go.

HER JAWS

Dreams are the land's long-distance hunters.
You can run over but you can never
run from the land.

The deer and I try,
but nightmares catch us
crossing Nevada's basin and range.

When I collapse into earth,
and let the dirt talk me into sleep,
an eagle flies through my insomnia.
She wraps her talons around my rib cage
and carries me to her nest.
Grieving, she cracks me open
and spills me over
the thin shells of her smashed eggs.

There are octopuses in my obsessions.
Salty and dehydrated,
they wash up dead
after being boiled alive.

The wise eyes of whales
watch to see what I'll do.
I can't decide if their tears
are oceans or oceans, tears.
And that's probably for the best
because I never want to know
what whales actually think of me.

Swimming, or weeping, all night,
in the sage brush sea,
when a mountain lion glides nearby.
Shadows part for her passing
and stars settle in her fur.

Beneath the fear of her selective gaze,
exhausted and nearly hypothermic,
with nothing but frost to kill the pain,

there is a longing the deer and I share,
a desire to be desired by her jaws tonight.

THE PLATTER

Ocean dreams tonight,
but I'm alone again in the desert.

I sink into sand,
the first beds for the first
weary bodies,
where our ancestors emerged
exhausted and dripping
to dry before the forests.

Sleep is cold.
I can only dip my toes in.
And when I do,
the sea speaks of something
deeper.

Waves nod and bump.
Their gentle push, their gentle pull
could carry me back
to where it all began
and where it all, thank god,
will end.

The flicker of fins in thickening foam
offers friendliness to soothe my loneliness.

Blood in the water
asks me if I'm mistaken.
My tips and corners

harden like shark's teeth
anticipating the euphoria
those teeth could flood me with
before transforming me
into sleek, predatory muscles
and wrapping my heart
in the grey armor
of rough shark skin.

As it is, my skin remains unprotected
and slowly reddens.
My eyes burn,
the ocean turns to acid,
and my own tides drag me away
until I wake again
dry, alive, and alone again
in this desert.

I feel ascetic up here
like I should be wearing
a camel hair shirt.
That, at least, would be
an itch I could figure out
how to scratch.

I had almost forgotten
that I'm not John the Baptist.
I don't know any ways to prepare,
the messiahs have all been dunked,

the honey has hardened,
and the locusts have left,

clearing my head for the platter.

And, when at last,
they force me to my knees,
stretch my neck over a stone,
and lift the axe, all I pray
is that I have the strength to say:

I much prefer the sharks.

THE ATTRACTION OF BONE TO STONE

Magic survives, but barely.
The machines don't need it.
They learned to suck blood from stones
long ago.

The sun, seeing everything, laments
and day falls all the hotter
from his weeping face.

Fleeing the sun's scorching tears,
I climb high into the Santa Rosas
until stones in the shade offer the only solace.

They watch for signs in the sky
with a patience trained
in the slowest wake of glaciers.

Their velocities are measured in millennia.
Their strength evident in irresistible expansions of ice.

When shovels and spades strike the stones' face,
canyons peal with echoes of shattered steel,
proving stones are too strong to turn the other cheek.

Together, the stones and I find
visions glimpsed thinly through the width
of a spider's silver thread twisting in the wind.

This glimmering slit, this slight crease in the blue,
gives the last, tiny view
of a portrait of the Earth as a young boulder.

Tectonic plates groan. The thread snaps.
The window slams shut.
And, the Earth and I are left world-weary again.

Yearning to match the pace of maturing minerals,
my spine finds a comfortable nook,
my hips sink into a strong chair, and my skull
rests on a granite pillow in the bedrock.

These ancient voices explain
that when the magic finally fails,
and the blood runs out,
I will succumb, at last,
to the attraction of bone to stone.

ONLY THE STONES

It was once a comfort to know,
one day, only the stones
will be left to remember.

Then I sat long enough with rocks
where a river used to run
before she was used up,
dried out,
spent

to buy the numbness
the broken whiskey bottles
and malt liquor cans represent.

I saw a snake's shedded skin
amongst the paper, plastic,
and glass that took
the freely flowing water's rightful place.

The stones whispered
as the snake skin brushed dust
from their dry, old faces.

With the snake skin's assistance,
the stones could see
the rusty robots
leaning on their shovels.

With all the minerals
finally ripped from all the mines,
the machines passed

their last barrel of oil around
and smoked what was left of their coal
like weed.

The exhausted machines
missed the connection
between the empty oil barrels
and broken whiskey bottles.

Only the stones will be left to remember.

And if a single snake skin survives
as miraculously long
as all the plastic,
the stones may recall
the fragments of reminiscences
of a long-dead river
on the last flicking tongue
of the last living snake's
dying hiss.

There will be no one left
to brush the dust away,
no one left to learn
that dust is tears
on a stone's face.

FIRST MEADOWLARK

Impatient Summer, blowing in hot,
scatters a continent's cries
before Spring knows anything is wrong.

The truth is hard to gather.
Smoke jaundices the sun's gaze
and convinces me that much more
than skin is burning.

Here in Nevada,
I listen to the sagebrush sea
listening to me.
I wonder if her diagnosis keeps her speechless,
if she's run out of things to say,
or if she's telling me that silence
is best between terminal friends.

Then, the year's first meadowlark.

He lights upon a sagebrush branch.
His proud, golden breast
reminds the Sun of her former, unblemished glory.
His voice mingles with March's first sunset
turning the air amber,
the color to preserve memories.

He sings forgotten songs,
the ones you feel long before you hear.

He puts the chill wind to bed.
Restless ghosts, drift on the breeze,
echoing his mortal lullabies,
until they finally fall asleep.

He hits a pitch, a sonic dagger,
that pierces my finest armor.
My bones hum. I begin to hear.

And, hearing, I weep.

The meadowlark sings the sounds
of a broken man and a beaten land
consoling themselves.

A CLOUD'S KISS

There are times
when waiting for the precise moment
rain freezes into snow
that the gray makes me wonder
if one more snow flake
broke the mountain's back.

If I leave too soon,
that's what happened.
One more was one too many
and turning my back on the horizon
to focus once more on smaller things
I know I'll never be as strong
as a mountain's granite spine.

It wasn't until I was sure
that one more really would be
one too many
that I turned my tears towards the storm.

Rain turned into snow
and a flake found the wrinkles
around my eyes.
A cloud kissed me there.
The lightest brush of her crystal lips
and her frosty tongue
turned my creases
made ever deeper by weeping
into smile lines.

And I knew a flake didn't break
the mountain's back.

The mountain shattered with the joy
that comes from being loved by the sky.

SONG (WHAT THE WORLD SOUNDS LIKE)

song
she calls it

but, four letters and a single syllable
make too weak a sound

for the original impossibility
made possible
when the seemingly eternal silence
proved only to be a multi-measure rest
interrupted by a Big Bang,
a cymbal crash,
and the staccato notes of atomic music

for letting us linger once more
in those safe spaces made by
the gentle beat of cottonwood seeds
coming to rest, at last,
in soothing tones of sunlight
floating down a mountain stream

for the warm hues of contralto blue
she paints on the dusken sky
sprinkled with the pure sweetness
of evening's first silver stars

for bringing ghosts to life
so we remember they're
dead

for helping us forget
with vanilla notes in caramel
and the perfect absence of smoke
when the bourbon
and our own voices run dry

for making us miss
what we never knew
was
      gone

WINTER, MY MISTRESS

The solstice came
but the winter did not.
So I asked my mistress
how she wanted to be loved.

She pulled me into a Colorado canyon
where her children, December's first snows,
huddled under shade and stones
to survive the unseasonable sunshine.

Hold me, she said, as close as snow
clings to shadow while the world burns.

She led me to a dried-up creek.
where, for millennia,
wet songs had once been sung.

Now, only silence flowed.
When wind dragged dust
and gravel across the creek bed,
we heard the creek
trying to clear her throat.

But, she was far too parched to sing.

Long for me, winter said,
like streams long for the music of water.
Use your tongue, she whispered,
to lick frost from the skin of the land.

Taste my ecstasy and paint my praises
on the howling north wind.

Resistance is my love language.
If you turn the heat down,
it will turn me on.

Kick the furnace.
Punch holes in pipes.
Fill the oil wells.
Always leave the tops on mountains.

And, when at last I come,
to give you chills and make you tremble,
don't be a fair-weather lover,
betraying me for warmth and comfort.

If you want me, you must choose:
Stand strong in the cold and
unsheathe your courage for me,

or bury your head in blankets and
unmask your impotency
for all the natural world to see.

RIVERBEDS

Waking once more in the gray
with my head on your bare chest,
the morning chill suggests
that the warmth we created last night
has flown away.

When the day beckons,
no matter how cold,
no matter how gray,
so long as your breast
holds me here in that certain way
that causes me to search
for the precise verb
holding rivers to their beds,

I just can't.

Sleeplessly searching,
all I recall is your brown eyes
the color of earth,
born as we all are from the dirt,
rooting you with that
blessed, grounded nature—

while mine are blue
and quick as water
to overflow and wash me away.

My dams threaten to break when you sigh.
Your dreams, your arms,
the loam in your instincts,
gather me in and pool me up.

And, I sleep again
knowing all rivers love their beds.

ANCIENT SUGAR

Remember when the moment flew away
shaking snow from pine boughs
and we stopped believing in time?

Horned owls sang. The notes of their tunes
tick-tock'd to announce the arrival of dusk.
You and I, shadows and dying light
were intertwined in the oldest way
to keep warm.

We disturbed some ants,
overwintering in our pine bed.
Your fingertips mimicked
tiny ant steps across my trembling skin.

When stillness settled over us, once again,
amber formed a golden sweat
on the tree's silver bark.
I asked you if you thought
we could get caught here,
forever fossilized in resin
under open skies.

Frozen starlight settled in your eyes.
You took the amber on your fingertips,
touched them like ancient sugar to our tongues,
and said, "It certainly tastes that way."

You taught me how to understand the owl song:
In the future, time will stop
and everyone else will all go on.

MY SPRING BREEZE LOVER

The spring breeze fills me with desire.
She swirls over my body
and there's nothing I can do
to hide it.

She pushes me gently
into a bed of warm April mud.
She sighs with the exquisite
trickling of melting snow.
When my lips part, to praise her,
she shows me dandelions.

Words, here, she whispers,
are dandelion sex.

Stalks bend in the wind,
their pale heads thoroughly blown
in the wake of her dancing.

I open myself like a book to her,
pages fluttering.
She pulls the ink from my skin
and scatters what I know
like small seeds across soft soil
damp with the desire to grow,
wet with the willingness to bloom.

But, of course,
I am not her only lover.
She has grasses to shake,

leaves to stir, birds to carry,
and fragrant news of the land's rebirth
to deliver.

She brushes the hair from my eyes,
kisses my eye lashes, and is gone.
I think the soil understands.
I ache to sprout forests for her
until she returns to me again.

FALLING FOR (AND FROM) THE SKY

It's hard not to fall in love
with the Nevada sky in May.

She kisses my pale skin
careful not to turn me
the color of her lips.

I blush anyway
and she laughs gently.
Her joy is the sound
of hummingbird wings
vibrating with satisfaction
at the discovery of hidden nectar.

She removes my sunglasses
so I can see her the way
she desires to be seen.
The ecstasy in my eyes
only encourages her.

I'm too shy to tell the sky
that I've always been proud
that my eyes are blue,
like her.

My heart throbs with longing
as she edges me closer to explosion
like a planet that ventures
too near the sun.

But just before she burns me,
when it's clear I can barely
stand her heat anymore,
she pulls the clouds over us,
and washes me with wind.

Her caressing zephyrs
teach me what my sweat is for.
When she gives me goosebumps,
the clouds part, and she begins
the bright cycle all over again.

As the sun sets,
and I feel her pulling away,
the sky reminds me
that this life is only a vapor.

"Evaporate for me,"
she whispers in my ear.
"And, we'll rise to shine
with the moon and stars."

But I know, if I was water,
and fell for and from the sky,
I'd only sprinkle like desert rain
after a lingering drought,
and never touch the ground.

YOUR FLOWER BLOOMING

The hummingbirds and the bees
taught me what my desire was for.

I was wingless until I flew
into the gift of your flower.
You showed me what to do.

My heart thrummed, my body buzzed,
and you taught me these vibrations
could help your flower bloom.

It would have been far more than enough
to bask in the perennial glory
in the unfurling of your blossom.
I would have been content to simply exist
in the sweet honor of playing my role.

But with petals opening around me,
burgeoning fragrances surrounding me,
and the flavor of your nectar on my tongue,

I discovered your joy growing with mine,
and intertwining our joys like this,
we could grow the most fruitful,
the most beautiful, the wildest gardens
with the purest fertilizer of all:

creating mutual pleasure together.

This must be why the little hummingbirds
fly so far, why the tiny bees work so hard.

They want to keep the flowers blooming.

LEG CRAMPS

Earth is not a voyeur.
It's just that she is everywhere.

She hates walls, fences, forts,
ceilings, and closed doors.
She rages against traps
and cages and anything
that isolates her children
from the open sky.

She was young once, too, you know,
and does her best to respect
the agreed upon talismans
hanging from locked door knobs.

She tries not to beckon us
by tickling damp sheets
with a delicious summer breeze.

She thought the thunder
might mask our music
and provide some sonic privacy.

Eventually, the storm passes on,
and there's nothing left
to hide dusk's summer stars
from settling in your smiling eyes.

So, we move outside,
to better see those stars,

to intertwine beneath tree trunks,
and create our own humidity.

When my legs cramp,
while your song remains unfinished,
Earth encourages me to endure.

Not because she's watching,
but because she's always teaching,
and some pains are worth facing

to help your beloved keep singing.

SUMMER RAIN EMBRACE

The land's breath,
as she sighed with the pleasure
of a sudden thunderstorm,
smelled like summer rain
and taught me isolation
is ever an illusion
encouraged by thirsty machines
and the insatiable hunger
hiding behind hot plastic screens.

The longing was real
even if it was enhanced by empty fantasy.
Summer's drought, the acrid taste
of fireworks, burning forests,
and the ensuing loneliness
left me starving for intimate tenderness.

But I was looking for love
in all the wrong places, the pretty faces
of total strangers
who I imagined smiled at me
— could she really have smiled at me?—
in the mirage of shimmering heat
dancing over brittle desert concrete.

The rain came and the land's perfume
drew me into her moist embrace.
Her hands, kind as cloud-softened sunshine,
cradled my aching head in the cool reassurance
offered by her breast.

Her fingers, skillful as the breeze,
stirred my dark hair and brushed
red burns from my shoulders and chest.

Before I could agonize over whether
my shoulders were broad enough,
my chest was strong enough,
my body desirable enough,
she kissed the fear and sweat
from my trembling skin
with gentle raindrops.

I do not know if the land's love
is the only kind of love I will ever need.
The distinction likely lacks any meaning
when every woman who has ever lived,
any woman who might ever love me,
is created as we all are
from the love given by the land.

I truly do not know.

In fact, all I really know
is after the summer rains finally fell,
the land held me
so cool, so close, so calm,
and so small in her arms,
that I finally fell asleep.

WHEN THAT SOMETHING
THAT WILL HAPPEN HAPPENS

This was the season that taught us
anything can happen,
and something will.

There's only so much you can do about it—
best to keep yourself open, available, watchful.
As far as we know, you only get to do this once,
after all.

Remember the time that has passed
and let it spice the times ahead.
Remember there are others,
the ones who are coming.
Let your time feed their time.
Let your time leave them with a better time.

Slow your own time down.
Hear the edges of the grains of sand
as they strike the hard surface
of the bottom of the hourglass.
Hold all that is lost as those grains pile up.
They will give the passing moments their fullness.

And, in this way,
when that something that will happen happens,
you'll be ready to do everything you can about it.

SNOWBANKS

When your soul is wobbly with vertigo,
drunk on the reality of nothing left to do,
step into the blizzard and listen to the snow.

Each flake is a whisper,
each drift a direction,
each pawprint someone who came before.

It will get cold.
There's no way to avoid it.
But, even the sun falls,
frozen wood eventually burns,
and the scent of smoke on the wind,
leads you somewhere.

If all these fail,
winter will numb you,
until you'll feel
only what she needs you to.

You might collapse onto snowbanks, then,
but you'll learn— yes, you'll learn
that snow is softer than bare stone.

MY MOTHER'S EYES

Thinking of my mother today
in this precise shade of afternoon blue
the color of her eyes.

while mine tend more towards dusk.

I settle back into earth
sharing delight
with a little boy stirring dust
with his running feet.

I have been here longer.

The strong sun discovers
deeper lines on my face
and my skin is coated
with thicker dust.

But I smile.

It feels good to remember
with this boy
where we come from

and where we're going.

It comes to me like this
watching my mother watching me
from far away and long ago.

I think she must have known.

WHAT WILL MY FATHERING BE?

A newborn baby girl in my arms,
her little head nestled against my chest.
She gazes into a world
that I must be too old now
to remember exists.

I'm not her father, never been a father,
never wanted to be a father.

But her precious, sharp fingernails
reach through my defenses
to find bare skin and she reminds me
of the urgency of her needs.

It's long been the urgency
of our Mother's needs
that has kept me from babies.

Then, I see
the blue planet in her blue eyes
locked now on mine.
And I know the planet's,
this baby girl's, and my needs
are the same.

She discovers the patchy beard on my face.

Fascinated by this new texture,
she scratches my cheek.
I want to flinch, push her hands away,
but I don't want to jostle
her small, rapidly expanding mind.

I know, then, that's what
my fathering will be.

I will hold Earth's children—

those bright minnows
gathering their courage to leave
the safe shade under stones
for the sunny currents downstream,

those downy, beak'd faces
poking through pale eggs
to feel the breeze
that will one day flutter
through fully-formed wings,

those yearling antelope,
stretching their skinny, quivering legs
before they learn just how fast
those legs will be,

and this little girl—

close to me.

I vow to be man— no— father enough
to face the pain that may come
from holding close
all Her many, many babies
without flinching away.

THE SCENT OF THIS PLACE

The land speaks
with gestures of instant significance.

Trees drop snow
in sudden tumbles of meaning.

Faded memories begin to glow,
rekindled in embers of fires
built to thaw frozen battlegrounds
before we dig in.

Magic walks the trapline with us.

Sometimes with the fox's straight, sure steps.
Sometimes with the wolverine's wandering trail.
Sometimes disappearing with the grouse's brushing wings.

At first, the words are simple echoes.
Voices from a distant fog— forgotten, but not inaudible.

At an empty trap,
we open the faded green, army surplus pack
to find leather and licorice,
castor, anise oil, fermented salmon eggs,
a little beaver meat, raspberry jam,
and the slightest tang of rum,
an original anti-freeze.

Then, while we smear
the blue marten lure on pine trunks,

color bleeds into clean white snow
and smells spill out.

We remember when he said
"the land gives you the words -
words to fall in love
with the scent of this place."

PRAYER FOR A PINE MARTEN

An old man's frost-flecked lips
flicker with the sky
as day dies in the west.

Sunshine tumbles
from cedar branches and pine needles
draping him in shadow.

His head is bowed, and kneeling in the snow,
his prayer lifts
crystalizes
with the steam of his breath.

Then, he meets her gaze.

The pewter stare of a trapped pine marten.

She's been waiting, patient despite the pain.
The rusted trap failed
to mercifully crush her breastbone.
So, she's been expecting him.

It seems to him,
as he presses her down,
that the strong heart beats in his thumbs
match the heart beats that fade in her chest.

And, the pulse of the universe feels like this.

ACKNOWLEDGMENTS

"When I Set the Sweetgrass Down" was published by *Braided Way Magazine*, Spring 2022.

"Someone Else's Map" was published in 2013-14 edition of the *San Diego Poetry Annual.*

"Winter, My Mistress" was published by Cathexis Northwest Press, February 2022.

"Snowbanks" was published by *Flying Island Journal* in March, 2021.

"Anthropocene Writer's Block," "This American Solstice," "A Dying Trickster's Last Joke," and "Nearly-Blind Rust Belt Blues," were published in the Spring 2022 edition of *The Wayfarer.*

ABOUT THE AUTHOR

Will Falk is a biophilic author, attorney, and activist. The natural world speaks and Falk's work is how he listens. He believes the intensifying destruction of the natural world is the most pressing issue confronting us today and he aims his writing at stopping this destruction. He is grateful to the places and countless creatures who have nurtured his writing. These include the Bayview shore of Lake Michigan in Milwaukee, WI; the *Unist'ot'en* Camp on unceded *Wet'suwet'en* land; sacred *Mauna Kea*; pinyon-juniper forests wherever they are found; the Colorado River; and *Peehee mu'huh* (Thacker Pass).

A former Wisconsin public defender, Falk's law practice is now devoted to protecting as much of the natural world as he can. His first book, *How Dams Fall*—a short work of creative nonfiction about his relationship with the Colorado River—was published as part of Homebound Publications' Little Bound Books series in 2019. Falk hopes his poetry will help his readers fall in love with the natural world and, once in love, to protect their beloved. You can follow Falk's work at willfalk.org.

HOMEBOUND
PUBLICATIONS

Since 2011 We are an award-winning independent publisher striving to ensure that the mainstream is not the only stream. More than a company, we are a community of writers and readers exploring the larger questions we face as a global village. It is our intention to preserve contemplative storytelling. We publish full-length introspective works of creative non-fiction, literary fiction, and poetry.

Look for Our Imprints Little Bound Books, Owl House Books, *The Wayfarer Magazine*, Wayfarer Books & Navigator Graphics

WWW.HOMEBOUNDPUBLICATIONS.COM

W A Y F A R E R

BASED IN THE BERKSHIRE MOUNTAINS, MASS.

The Wayfarer Magazine. Since 2012, *The Wayfarer* has been offering literature, interviews, and art with the intention to inspires our readers, enrich their lives, and highlight the power for agency and change-making that each individual holds. By our definition, a wayfarer is one whose inner-compass is ever-oriented to truth, wisdom, healing, and beauty in their own wandering. *The Wayfarer's* mission as a publication is to foster a community of contemplative voices and provide readers with resources and perspectives that support them in their own journey.

Wayfarer Books is our newest imprint! After nearly 10 years in print, *The Wayfarer Magazine* is branching out from our magazine to become a full-fledged publishing house offering full-length works of eco-literature!

Wayfarer Farm & Retreat is our latest endeavor, springing up in the Berkshire Mountains of Massachusetts. Set to open to the public in 2025, the 15-acre retreat will offer workshops, farm-to-table dinners, off-grid retreat cabins, and artist residencies.

WWW.WAYFARERBOOKS.ORG

www.ingramcontent.com/pod-product-compliance
Lightning Source LLC
Chambersburg PA
CBHW052112020426
42335CB00021B/2730